TALKING SANSKRIT TO FALLEN LEAVES

to
Roland John
with good wishes
Satyendra
21/2/98

TALKING SANSKRIT TO FALLEN LEAVES

SATYENDRA SRIVASTAVA

PEEPAL TREE

First published in Great Britain in 1994 by
Peepal Tree Books
17 King's Avenue
Leeds LS6 1QS
England

© Satyendra Srivastava 1994

All rights reserved
No part of this publication may be
reproduced or transmitted in any form
without permission

ISBN 0 948833 66 1

ACKNOWLEDGEMENTS

Acknowledgements are due to the editors of the following in which some of the poems first appeared:
Ambit, Iron, Poetry Digest, Verse, Nutshell, The Pathway, The Spectator, Smiths Knoll, Illuminations, Planet International, Hybrid, New Spokes, Exile, The Haiku Quarterly, Dial 174, Paris Atlantic, Trinidad Guardian, New Hope International, Wasafiri, Quartos Magazine and *Understanding*.

A very special thanks to Di Gough for helping in the preparation of the typescript, her constructive criticism and encouragement.

CONTENTS

The Silent Buddha	9
Windows	11
Habitual Helplessness	12
The Ticket	13
Memory	14
The Children of the Blood Game	15
Do as I Tell You	16
The Killing of Mrs Broody	17
Making Love in Common Waters	19
The Depth of Surface	20
Bob Shillington Plays Cricket Alone	21
Palms	24
Prajapati's Question	25
The Second Skin	26
Indifferent	27
Talking Sanskrit to Fallen Leaves	29
The Survival of Together	30
Lollipop Love	31
The Tiger	32
Second Time	34
A Dessert Song	35
Traditions Continue	36
The Interval of a Roman Emperor	37
Celebrating a Birthday	39
At the Funeral of Tom Dickensworth	40
In Ma's Bosom	41
Ancestral Cobra	44
The Glacier Baby	46
The Twilight Mother	48
The Nightingale Sings	50
Through Bhasmlochan's Eyes	51
At the Middle of the Bridge	53
A Midnight Sacrifice	54

On the Sun Island	56
The Bhasmasur Love	58
The Noble Torturer	60
Solutions	61
Arrival of a Galloping Horseman	62
The Silence	63
The Life Cycle	64
Poems	65
Beating the Dead	66
The Days are Flying Away	67
On Returning Home	68
The Banana Tree in front of the Window	69
Losing My Swastika	70
The Kites	72
A View of the World from a Half-Open Window	73
Observing Gravity	74
The Resolve	75

THE SILENT BUDDHA

The good old Buddha
He witnessed them all
With his eyes closed
His feet lotus-folded
His lips smiling
His palm blessing
Because he couldn't help
He was right there
Right in front
On the mental peace
He saw it all
With sure impassive face
The dance of shining-firm round handsome hips
Creating havoc
On the mosaic of a soft rug on the pucca floor
The fucks like hell
And the fucks of a lifetime
He witnessed them all
With silence
All alone
Without clapping
Without bucking anybody up
He had seen in his lifetime
Homeless men, shivering and begging in streets
But perhaps not this one night flip
A rich, well-dressed lady
inviting a handsome young
homeless boy to her home
On the floor
And the rug
To go into her everywhere

With the ever increasing sound of a drum beat
The hi-fi sound penetrating the sky
And the sandalwood incense
Intoxicating every move
All that happened and happened so beautifully
So powerfully
Because the desire was there and the chance
The good old Buddha
No disrespect to you, Sir
But I would say this
Desire is not the root of all the troubles
In here it is of joy
And that can be anywhere
If the time is ripe
And the willingness is there
And the hunger is immense

WINDOWS

Mama used to say
Son these are your eyes
These are your windows
In every glance
Try to see something beyond
Something beyond
What there is
When a dog wipes the floor
Where he sits
It doesn't amaze you any more
You know what he is up to
Yet he is telling us something
When the cat taps your finger
To draw your attention
She is not necessarily hungry
Maybe she wants you to touch her
She wants to make the distance
Of even the skins disappear

Mama was right
She has gone
I open my eyes
And look beyond
And there she is
Every time telling me
Open them a little more my love
A little more
And you will find still more
And more

HABITUAL HELPLESSNESS

Again
The wind rattles
On a blank paper
Songs in the making
My fingertips
Lying solemn on a pincushion
Feel the warmth of their sharpness
Penetrating the skin
The music must not stop
The blue air messages
Shifting the time-scale
On a distant trumpet
Must go on
This
For you is a daily practice —
For me listening to it
Is an habitual helplessness

THE TICKET

Hold tight
Any more fares please
Called the conductor
Heathrow Terminal 4 please
Said a sari-clad passenger
It's one way isn't it Madam
Asked the conductor
No it's return really
But you can't give that can you
Said the lady
No I can't Madam
But I will gladly give you one way
Replied the conductor
The woman kept quiet
Just offered the fare
The conductor took it
Gave her the ticket
And then looked at the smiling elderly lady
Sitting behind
And gave her a wink

MEMORY

It is that moment
When you hear voices
And after pondering a while
Realise that there aren't any
And you feel cheated

It's that shape
Which you know is a void
Even though you want to paint it
But feel helpless

It's that feeling
When you are contented
Enjoying the vast spread in front
And then suddenly hear a cry
Don't move
The sea is rough
And the whale's gone crazy
Don't turn back either
The town is on fire
And you feel trapped

This is the way
I describe
Memory

THE CHILDREN OF THE BLOOD GAME

The trigger-happy soldiers
Are not the only chosen people
On this often thirsty ground
We are all children of the blood game
For all of us
Somewhere
An enemy exists
Real or otherwise
All of us carry a gun
Visible or hidden
Bearing it on our shoulders
Or mostly on others
Waiting to shoot
When we fail to achieve
What we went for or
Whenever illusions shatter
And dreams are broken

DO AS I TELL YOU

For the children of Bosnia
It was a new method of learning English
The young blond teacher
While explaining the idiom
Do as I tell you
Stopped for a few moments
And looked
Across the class
With unseeing eyes
And unzipped her trousers
Took off her pants
Threw herself on the floor
With no emotion
And told the class
In this country when soldiers come
And shout
Do as I tell you
This is what you do

THE KILLING OF MRS BROODY

The killing of Mrs Broody was
Not a revenge
Yet it was a cold-blooded murder
In a sense it was more so because
While I was doing it
I was fully aware that
Those hands which were killing Mrs Broody
Were not those of a devil that had taken abode
In me and was making me do it
The killer's hands were definitely mine
And they knew what they were up to
And I for once felt
I can accomplish things if I set my mind to it

That's why I satisfactorily and
Somehow boldly told those buggers
About my dream in which I had
Murdered Mrs Broody
One of them that Nick Orwell thereupon
Not only jumped on his chair with joy
But a little later phoned Mrs Broody
About my killing
He thought this will win her over

But she knew the game
And told him bluntly
Killing me in a dream sounds more honourable
Than being masturbated on
Nick darling

My God Mrs Broody although
Well in her forties is really something
But then she has been known for putting men
In their place

I'm now doubly sure that
I did not kill Mrs Broody for any revenge

MAKING LOVE IN COMMON WATERS

The point wasn't that they didn't possess
Any social conscience
It wasn't that all
The looming threats
Of wars and conflicts
The ever rising percentages
Of thefts rapes murders burglaries
Didn't touch them
It wasn't that they didn't give a shit
Who became president prime minister
Chancellor or martial law administrator
They simply thought it was all like clockwork
That all this had to be
That it was in the nature of things
That men will commit crime
And make a mess to survive
That however loudly the ideals are announced
Machiavelli's prince is bound to emerge
So
When they had bribed the caretaker
To look the other way
And after all the swimmers had gone
They made love
In the common waters
They did not do it
To prove that they were different
But they felt that by making love
In the dirt of others
They were purifying the water
And themselves too

THE DEPTH OF THE SURFACE

Into the icy
Cold quiet surface
Of the water
Slowly
Putting my palms and
Keeping them there
For a while
I realised suddenly
That surface
Has a depth too

BOB SHILLINGTON PLAYS CRICKET ALONE

Bob Shillington plays cricket alone
Bob Shillington, whose white and grey hair is blown all
                                                  over
Who wears three woollen coats even in the heat
Who, just got up from sleep
Empties the last of last night's wine into his belly
Folds the cardboard box which is his bed and bedding
Puts it in a corner
Abuses one or two passers-by
Now, with the help of an unfinished wall,
Is playing cricket
Bob Shillington in his hands
Takes a foot and a half long thin stick
And holding it firmly, moving it up and down, lifting it sky
                                                  high

Is now batting
Bob Shillington
Lifting his bat a little higher
Is shouting
    Throw!
    Bastards! Throw all
    Throw one by one
    Throw fast
    Throw slow
    Throw a googly
    I will hit every ball
    Hit each and every one of them
    I will hit a four
    Hit a sixer
    Hit all
    Hit each and every one!

Bob Shillington is shouting
And playing cricket.
Bob Shillington is also feeling
That nobody is bowling
No one is throwing the ball from any side
After a while
Bob Shillington keeps his bat by the stumps of the bricks
And observing the people coming and going
Sometimes he laughs
And at times abuses

Bob Shillington just saw an Asian
Bob Shillington stopped him
Asked him for money for tea
And was turned down with cool Asian politeness
The Asian went and Bob Shillington kept looking at him
A few moments
Then he shouted
    You! Son of a bitch!
    Come unwanted here
    Eat our bread
    And do not give us money!

Then Bob Shillington becomes quiet
And lifts his bat, offering it on all sides
Keeps batting
Keeps abusing
Bob Shillington abuses all
Except the children
Boys sometimes throw stones, banana peels or other things
                                        at him

Or go near him

Keep their handkerchiefs to their noses
And spit on his smelly coat
Even then
Bob Shillington utters not a word
Only laughs
And when they go away
Then he shouts
    All will go! When the time comes all will go
    All will pass unchanged
    Just as Peter went, open-mouthed, hands flung
    Used to call himself a captain before me
    All will go! Yes, yes, all will leave
    As Hitler went, Stalin went
    As Major Livingstone went
    Wanted to bowl me out, the rascal, betrayer
    Yes, yes, all will go, one by one all will go
    As Maggie went, Mother Theresa will go —
    Came here
    Calling London a Calcutta!

Every day
Even today
Bob Shillington is playing cricket alone
Hitting hard and strong
Shouting loud and long, abusing
Throw!
Bastards throw!
Throw hard
Throw slow
Throw a googly
Throw
Throw with all your might!

PALMS

My one palm greets
The other
Like mirrors they face
Each other
Like mirrors they reflect
In each other
And my finger tips
Blink, tell their stories
Speak the language of touches
They boast
Of calming overburdened feelings
Of arousing suppressed desires
Of turning into fists when
Time to attack
They talk of how
They touched the feet
And begged
And even how they remain
Uselessly open
Like resigned and abandoned horizons
Only a *namastey*
Stops them chatting
Brings them together

PRAJAPATI'S QUESTION

In the beginning
A Hindu scripture says
The earth was bare
There existed neither plants nor trees
Prajapati — the lord of creatures —
Creator and supporter of the universe
Once asked himself
How he could have descendants
After torturing and mortifying himself
He eventually produced flaming Agni
From his mouth
And because Agni came
Out of his mouth
He became a consumer of food
Then Prajapati realised that
Although he had made a food consumer
There was no food for him
Indeed on this earth
There was no edible object
Other than Prajapati himself
Prajapati then asked
In that case
Would not Agni eat him up...

This burning question
Has haunted man
Thereafter

THE SECOND SKIN

This one is not
The Sita of *Ramayana*
Nor from Ayodhya
She is Sita from Chapel Street
Hounslow Middlesex sick with
Chronic heart disease
When the nurse asked her to change
Into something more comfortable
Sita replied
This is the most comfortable thing
I have, next to my skin
The sari is my second skin
I would like to die wearing it
It is my *pahchan* my identity
Her husband standing nearby
Smiled happily and told the nurse
My dear
Not very long ago
But certainly long before you were born
Some strange Englishmen went to India
They wanted to turn Indians into
Dark coloured Brits
But they miserably failed
You know why
Because the Sitas of India
Like this one
Never discarded
Their second skin

INDIFFERENT

This isn't my country
Because it isn't
Because this has a name
A geography
Flora and fauna
Landscape
Houses shops people
This isn't my island
Because it isn't
Because here the water is rough
Waves are challenging
Trees are green
The plants fresh
The rocks high and belittling
Skyscrapers threatening
This isn't my house
Because it isn't
Here no footsteps follow me around
The silence does not remind me of
People long gone away
The pictures on the wall don't speak
Don't have language
This isn't my room
Because it isn't
Because it is bright
Anyone can come in
Without knocking on the door
Through the windows and holes
Like sun with all its glamour and shine
Moon with mysteries
Wind with messages

Darkness with fear
Tense silence with provocation
This isn't my bed
Because it isn't
Because it is warm
Because it is inviting

TALKING SANSKRIT TO FALLEN LEAVES

Talking Sanskrit
To fallen leaves
Awakens in my inner solitude
A poet of Kalidasa's stature —
I have spoken in my silence
Countless megdoots and
Shakuntalas:
The empty clouds have listened to
My drowning messages
And shakuntalas have opened up
The eternities of my desires
But I did not do what
The great poet did once in his
Woodland
Chop the tree's branch he was sitting on
Nobody calls that genius a loony
But what should I call these
Who in the veil of night come and
Chop up everything
Poetry and all
Leaving dried-up leaves
To tell the stories
This time not in Sanskrit
But in everyone's language

Tears

THE SURVIVAL OF TOGETHER

In the Mahabharata
The ocean asks a river
How come
You bring mighty trees to me
But never the thin
Weak reeds
The river replies
The trees stand firmly rooted
Cannot bear the onslaught
Of my force for long
But the reeds bend
And move
According to the currents
That's why...

I wonder
If today we need
The spirit of the reeds
In our homes even more than
On the battlefields

LOLLIPOP LOVE

The sucking of a lollipop
When she sits on top
And makes love
Opens up every taste bud
Pink and melon red
Like long legs
Stretching to eternity
And then
The milk of her desires
Dripping from her eyes and
Tongue rolling on the wet lips
Turns into a warm
Running stream
On her chest
And after merging into
Her sweat and shouts
Pours down
Into the lollipop
Sharpening its tangy sweetness
Enhancing
The thirst of whetted desires

THE TIGER

When to the rhythm of
Her finger clicks she sings
There is a tiger in my tank
There is
Then asking Rita anything
Is asking for it
But I did
I asked her if the new born baby
Inherited her deep brown ocean eyes
The baby's sure got my black skin she said
What about eyes
I bet she has I said
Go and see for yourself
The nurse won't mind
She said again clicking her fingers
I went to the babies' room in Stevens Ward
Babies were crying
Perhaps it was feeding time
I returned to Rita
Before I sat down near her bed she asked
So what did you find
I said I didn't see
All the babies yellow white black brown
Were crying
Perhaps it was feeding time
And babies' cries don't reveal their colour
Rita smiled
Began to click her fingers again
And started humming

That's what I mean
That's what I mean
And she went on rhyming and clicking
There is a tiger in my tank
There sure is

SECOND TIME

The jaguar look in those
big black sharp eyes had
done it. The middle-aged

fat-bellied man enjoyed it
all the way, and while
rubbing his sweat-dripping

body with cologne-dipped
towel asked her how much
for a second time. She

curtly replied same no
concessions. He smiled
said you are good at it

you know. I'll go for the
second. And added you are
such a stunning Asian girl

anybody would marry you and
drive you around in a jaguar
She replied my husband

drives a jaguar. This I do to
kill my mother-in-law slowly
and her shame for me. Because

she still taunts me that my
father did not pay the
agreed dowry

A DESSERT SONG

The epilogue
Of the pre-theatre set menu
The four soft green figs
Dipped in liqueur and syrup
And layers of cream
In a transparent
Flowery Venetian glass
Dessert dish
The crowded tavern's
Dance of candle light
To a popular Sicilian tune
Suddenly the dark-eyed Arab girl
Spoke quietly
Into my hungry looks:
In Hebrew *Teenah* means
To spread out
The Hebrew concept of peace
Was to sit under
One's own fig tree...
Then she paused for two seconds
Took a deep breath
And repeated
The word 'own'
With a torn smile
And after another pause
She quickly picked out
The darkest fig
From the dessert dish
And gulped it down
Abruptly
The popular Sicilian tavern song
Had hit
The second note

TRADITIONS CONTINUE

Millennia ago
In a forest
A pair of curlews were hopping
On the grass
Singing the sweetest melody
When appeared a cruel fowler
And with one swift blow
Stilled the male bird
The bird fell and
Weltering in its blood
Died instantly
The mate began to mourn
In a pitiful tone
A poet strolling by saw it all
With deepest pity and sorrow
Uttered a curse on the fowler
The curse when expressed
Took the form of a poem
We still recite that poem
We still relish blood games

THE INTERVAL OF A ROMAN EMPEROR

On a simple moonlit night
When the moon was not telling stories
And the children had already heard theirs
And had gone to sleep
The name of a Roman emperor was murmured
The burning of a whole colony was enacted
A whistle, a song, the tinkling of a harp
And roaring lions appeared
People saw their mighty teeth
Getting into the first Christians
A crude nightmarish scream burst open like a wound
And the dirty red blood began to flow
Right at this moment he started his unending journey
On the dingy room's green carpet ten by ten
He began with a slow march
As if a head of state was taking the marching salute
Then he hastened his pace
He went faster and faster
Especially towards the north
Where the window was wide open
Inviting the moon to the silence of darkness
Today his face was bright
Like the therapeutic rays of the moonlight
A smile fixed not dead
Today he did not sing
He just kept on walking
North to south then south to east
And lastly to the west
After miles of journeying through thundery time scales
He stopped and picked a knife
The Mata Hari act was about to begin (his version)

It was only then that the first stone
Was hurled at the window
In the end he did not kill himself
Neither did the stone kill him
Yet he felt the game was over
Unashamedly he began to sing
And went on and on and on

In the morning
The cleaning lady again found him asleep
On the green carpet
Lying flat on his chest clenching a piece of paper
His toothless jaw open

CELEBRATING A BIRTHDAY

If things could have stayed
As they were
Longing to change
Into Utopias
If what was held closest to the chest
So tightly
Could come back
The talks repeat themselves
If life could be relived
One more mercury dream
If the words could express
In colours rather than layers
Today
I would have lit the candles
To celebrate
This one more passing year

AT THE FUNERAL OF TOM DICKINSWORTH

At Tom's funeral
Everybody said something
And whatever they said
Said it loudly
Old Uncle Fred said
Tom was stubborn
But never unreasonable
Aunt Sally opined
I watched him grow
And what a lad he grew into
The publican Wilfred said
He was the only regular
Who never asked for credit
But the loudest was
His younger brother Bill who said
We fought all the way
On everything and on every issue
But he never fought dirty
Tom's widow Violet
Remained quiet for a long time
Then she suddenly moved slowly
To her right
And whispered in the ear
Of her best friend Rose
Are we at the right grave darling

IN MA'S BOSOM

The shiny brown pointed
Fingers of Gauri the
Herdsmen's little princess
Have known the touches of her cow Radha's
Full firm udder and
The music of milk spurts
That flows from it
Into the tin bucket:
Trin trin tra
Tra tra trin trin
Familiar to her also are the railway tracks
Passing near the village
And stretching to eternity
Encompassing the *Prithvi ma*—
The earth goddess
Her land is thus linked with
The wide world up there
Every morning a local train comes to collect
All the milk containers from the village
To take away to distant lands
To feed serve and protect
The children of *Prithvi ma*
And for her this land whose
Sweet grass Radha eats and
Whose milk feeds the children of the world
Is safe because
The eternal shadow of Mount Goverdhan
Is spread there like an enormous umbrella
Once raised by Krishna on his one finger
To protect these herdsmen's land
And their cattle from the onslaught of demons

To destroy the earth
Hence all talk of acid rain sulphur heat
Environmental pollution etc had remained
So far vague foreign and distant for her
But today on returning to her open patch
She found Radha's eyes — the eponymous objects
Of unusual beauty — bloodshot
And her familiar
Cream white pure virgin milk
Always cloaked in a fragrance of
Fresh grass and honey had
Turned into sheets of liquid mud
Panicked Gauri felt that Radha was sick
Ran to the local vet
Who came at once and examined
Confided nothing was wrong with the cow
It was the polluted air that had
Dripped acid into Radha's eyes and
Contaminated the milk colour
The shock of the news
Threw the princess off balance
Her vision of the world
Began to reflect the turmoil of
Primeval demonic storms
Encircling all she dearly possessed
She threw herself on the ground
And embracing the earth began to cry
O *Prithvi ma* you are a warm
And nourishing goddess
You provide substance to all
Who move upon you

You pour out your milk for us
Ma save us from the holocaust
Radha watched Gauri's plight with bloodshot
And crying eyes

The vet had never seen such helplessness
Such despair
In any creature's eyes
Before

ANCESTRAL COBRA

For the children of Nagpuri
The cobra did not have
Any ancestral value
Yet the womenfolk left
A bowl of sweet milk every night
Near the women's bathing place
And the children's curiosity
Took them at the crack of every dawn
To find out if the snakes had come
And drunk the milk
In the night
And after finding the milk still
Unconsumed they laughed
And taunted their mothers
Why do you waste milk like this, Mummy?
There aren't any cobras now
They are all dead
History kaput
My mother with wet tears
And rolling eyes thereupon would only say
My dearest you don't understand
You are not a mother
A mother knows the pain of carrying
A child in her womb for nine months
In this old village one mother
Carried a cobra baby as I carried you
That mother was bathing right there
A cobra passed by
She panicked
Folded her palms and prayed
O cobra please don't hurt me

The cobra stood erect for a moment
And looked at her as if spellbound by her beauty
Spat out a white liquid that fell
Almost between her legs
Nine months later she gave birth to a cobra baby
In this family by providing milk
We say to the world that babies are babies
Human or cobra

THE GLACIER BABY

They kept in touch
Like Himalayan glaciers
Overspilling from the mountain's topknot
Into the bosom of earth's tranquillity
Like the *papi pet*, the
Hungry stomach compels
The mortals to melt and move

They came down in water drips
Drop by drop
With parting tears and
Fell into the fat man's kingdom

The cold stream with
A rhythm and movement
Of its own
Then registered the undercurrents
The silent words
The motionless journeys
The commitments through lip-sealed interpreters
Clearly expressed
And silently understood

Our *bulla* — the hill-billy
To us children
The sturdiest worker
The dreamer the toymaker
The disciplinarian even the governor
Working for thirty rupees a month
Reflected the essence of glacier movements

He one day proudly announced
That he had become a daddy
How come?
Asked my naughty sister
You haven't seen her for two years

The *bulla* replied
Standing erect
But we correspond
Our words our silent messages —
Less said more understood —
Carefully inscribed by the letter writer
Have always been taken in well
Like the mountain river

My sister smiled
Quickly changed the subject
And exclaimed
Never mind
Here comes the new one
To share the burden of India's other
Eight hundred million
Let us rejoice
At the birth of our nation's
Glacier baby

THE TWILIGHT MOTHER

When the sun ripens
And twilight falls on
This sleeping Bombay ghetto
She begins her walk
Into the empty side streets
End to end

She walks happily
With all her children
Her arms wrapped around them
Keeping intact all the grandeur
Of motherhood
Avoiding the glances of
Chatting street vendors and
The shadows of drug peddlers
And the like skulking
In their hiding places

She strolls without
Transmitting any messages
And
Like every twice born
High-caste Hindu explains
To her children
The significance of their names
Arjuna — for bravery
Generosity and friendship
Hanuman — for devoted service and loyalty
Laxami — for wealth and good luck

After the walk
And buying the packed meal
She returns
Gives her children their share
And after the meal
Kisses them goodbye and
Orders them to go to the
Other side of the curtain and sleep
Until they are woken up again
Reminding them sternly
Never to peep from the curtain
Never to move even if
They hear the sound of beating
Whipping crying or
Very loud laughter

Then moving the other little curtain
She goes to the wash basin
Washes herself
Offers her prayers in front
Of pictures of Arjuna Hanuman Laxami
Stuck over the pipe
And then takes off her bra
And her petticoat and
Wearing a thin pink nylon sari
She comes out
Sits herself down on the little stool
And after uttering
God's first word *om*
She starts to relive once more
Her daily routine
Her fame her skill
And her pride

THE NIGHTINGALE SINGS

She was told that the nightingale
sings in Berkeley Square. She was
told this by her English teacher and

the London-born Rakesh too. So the
proposal of marriage was accepted
at once. Father was lured so was she

House of her own in Belsize Park
Carpet wall to wall TV and video
dishwasher and tumble dryer and

what not. Newly wed Anjali left
the village for the promised land
and on arrival found the task of

sharing. Working for the mortgage
washing machine still to be paid for,
a new life began in a department

store in Oxford Street. And
while vacuuming the office and
cleaning out the ladies' she

looks across the street to Berkeley
Square humming to an Indian tune the words
the nightingale sings ...

THROUGH BHASMLOCHAN'S EYES

My mentor used to say
In the layers of a mirror
Parallel images create
Reflections
In it even mercury
Can draw its own replicas
My mentor also said that
Soon after getting up from sleep
The first thing a wise man should do
Is to look at his own face in the mirror
And smile
This will set him up for the day

I began
To follow his advice

Many many years later
When my mentor had become old
And without much eyesight
He told me the story of Bhasmlochan
He said this demon was blessed with the power
Of burning anyone
By just looking at him
One day
A treacherous friend put a mirror
In front of the demon
The demon looked into the mirror
Saw his own image in it
And was burnt instantly

After this story
My mentor paused for a moment
Looked at me through his thick glasses
Smiled
And said
I am really glad to see you

AT THE MIDDLE OF THE BRIDGE

When we had crossed
Half the bridge
Then the Sherpa spoke
The lions which once roared
On the peaks are no longer there
Now someone has dug in
A flag
The Sherpa says
Now no lion will
Wander there
If he comes, it will
Change to a root
Then perhaps a tree
And in course of time, a stone
The Himalaya was not always
Like this
Whatever has come up on this earth
Is the result of foundation and addition
The Sherpa says
The flag too will not always remain so
A gust of wind will uproot it
And cause it to become
Part of the mountain layers
This is the story of
The progress of this creation
This is what the Sherpa said
When we had crossed half the bridge

A MIDNIGHT SACRIFICE

In the flickering candlelight
For the third time
He rubbed his back hard and repeatedly
Against the rough bark of the old oak tree
Aware of the blood stain on his back
He touched it with one finger
And swiftly sucked a few drops
He snuffed the candle
Threw himself on the ground
Embracing the earth in his outstretched arms
He began to hit his head
On the stone roots of the tree
Now he had awakened the deity
A motionless silence followed
A dark magnetic pull of his inner self began
He joyfully realised that
He had rescued some broken skeletons
He began to draw their pictures
On the void in front
The skeletons assumed names
Identity and rituals followed
He narrated the story of their deaths and rebirths
Chanting their glory
And realising that he had freed them
He felt himself emancipated
He began to see the silence all around
Spreading on the cool lake of rose-petalled water
He began to swim in it
Halfway he stopped and took a dive
Re-emerged

And in the loudest possible voice he shouted
I have found it at last
Here it is
Here is the rainbow
Standing in waist deep water he then showed
It to the universe
Then took another dive
And never came up

On the ripples thereafter
A name appeared
But no-one could read it

ON THE SUN ISLAND

On the sun island
Trees were burned dead
Time stood like bald rocks
Plants had their last rites performed
The glory of love had outlived its meaning
Manoeuvring hope against hope
For a long time those maddening fragments of emptiness
Kept on encircling everything
Even engulfed the limits of ozone layers
And then the butchers came
Their hands up declaring they could not carry out the
    executions
The offenders were already dead
And the carcasses rotten
The butchers kicked themselves again and again
That feeling of dry hollowness that demeaned their manly
    existence
And wounded morale
However not everything was dead
Near the Y rock
Some men still shouted slogans
And their women were bare
Showing their wounded bellies
Pointing to the blue marks on their wounded intestines
They were all crying their eyes out
They all said they tried their very best to smoothe the births
But the babies refused to come out
So they failed
And abortions of the dead were performed
Since then no prophet has ever been born on the sun island

Now here in the deepening nights
Only two dogs bark
One claiming to be the god
The other his devil
In fact they are neither of these
They are simply dog-shaped shadows of two empty rocks
Rocks of the sun island

THE BHASMASUR LOVE

Bone to bone
Blood to blood
Limb to limbs
As if they were glued.
— Merseburg magic maxims

When love
Reaches its climax
— when it really does
It attains the ultimate
It could even perform
The final act
It could become a Bhasmasur
And burn itself to ashes
Like the demon himself
Who through great meditation
And sacrifice
Got the blessing of the god Shiva
And the power to burn anyone
By just putting his hand
On the person's head

Drunk with his power and love
He became infatuated
Almost obsessed
With the love of god Shiva's consort
And that was it
The other gods saw in this madness
In this love of a demon
For the goddess Parvati

A peril
Which must be averted
They plotted against him and
Somehow tricked him into
Putting his hand on his own head
And that's what he did
And that's how
He burned himself alive

So goes the story of Bhasmasur
It could be the story of love too

THE NOBLE TORTURER

With positive thinking
You can cross the Atlantic
On a haycock, says a Norwegian
The advice echoes
The sleeping valley
Recovering from a state of shock
Begins to hum in the language of birds and breezes
In the mosquito net of morning haze
Lying here is the King
The sentries watch the smugglers' chess games
Up there the men in uniform
Have taken their position ready to shoot
They talk of their days in bunkers
They have accounts to settle
The valley looks like
A killing field in the making
With positive thinking
You can cross the Atlantic on a haycock
And we will
We live on
Observing
Here no explanation is sought
None ever given
We are the witnesses of happenings
In a world of our own creation
Where the King sleeps
He will rise one day
And might lead us
To the Promised Land
Positively

SOLUTIONS

There are no solutions
There are men and women
And he animals and she animals
And he nature and she nature
And we have a spark
An urge
And the passion to create
We are all right here
Solutions

What for?

ARRIVAL OF A GALLOPING HORSEMAN

That galloping horseman
Jumping over the statue
Of St X
Arrived at my door
And put on my palm
A yellowed paper
With only a few figures
21.3.93
Jotted on it
And went back
As if never to return
But I know he will
With another text

THE SILENCE

This deafening silence
I thought I had escaped
The chain of rebirths
Of not
Remembering
But this silence is repeating itself
Like an uncontrollable ocean
Silences have a way
Of undoing you systematically
And conclusively
Layer by layer and
Sigh by sigh

THE LIFE CYCLE

This life
Is a rebirth
In every passing moment
On the cycles of death
Is erected a vertical ladder
And shadows hang
On the horizontal voids
This is the cross
Here I am

From me to you
An empty sealed envelope
A message of silent suffering

Throw your angry word arrows
I am like a dartboard
Never big enough for you

In the autumn sky
A red moon rages
Over dead fires

BEATING THE DEAD

Holding a stick in my hand
I am making a return journey
On a familiar path
Here in every stone-eyed
Curled-up dead snake
I read the words
Love once was

THE DAYS ARE FLYING AWAY

The days are flying away
Like the fading colours of the wall
Time is disappearing
First went the shine
Blotches of water began to show
Cracks opened up
The dark bricks revealed their
Ugly presence
What should we do
Start rubbing our hands
Or beat our heavy chests
Nothing
Let them go
Keep on meditating
Keep gazing
Gather the light
Scattered in the valley of vision
Sad days, departing
Let them go

ON RETURNING HOME

Every return journey home
Is an unfinished sentence
Uttered in anger
The immaculate silence meditating
Doors open
Like haikus
The silence of bedroom
Still greets
A geisha girl
Bowing and touching
The senses
Until reclaimed by deathly sleep

THE BANANA TREE IN FRONT OF THE WINDOW

The peeling of the banana tree
Was not a ritual here
And so it remained standing
Right in front of the double-glazed window
On top of the window
Was the inscribed motto:
As there are leaves within the leaves
Of a banana tree
There is a sense within a sense
Of a wise man's talk
But here no-one talked
The silence ruled
And the banana tree watched
And absorbed all the quiet
And the sobs and tears
And anger and helplessness

On the twelfth night of the moon
He fulfilled his vow
And offered the sacrifice
The banana tree was cut and
Laid on the ground as a sacrificial gift
But no-one accepted the offer
And the tree lay there for weeks

Then he began to peel its layers
One by one
And leaf by leaf
Right to the end
And he reached the point
Where there was nothing left to peel
And he felt
He had arrived

LOSING MY SWASTIKA

It was a pious gesture
A saffron coloured swastika
Embroidered on a silk handkerchief —
A Hindu symbol of Om
For an auspicious beginning —
Tucked in my pocket by the eldest aunt
On leaving Bombay harbour

In London I put it with old clothes
In a suitcase
And forgot all about it

Until one day
My hands dug deep into
The old suitcase and pulled out
The swastika-embroidered silk handkerchief
To wipe away the sweat the anger
And the frustration
After Enoch Powell's
Bloodbath speech

That was some twenty years ago
And then I changed house
And habits
No silk handkerchief now
Paper hankies do

Now in 1993
I am desperately searching for it
To explain to the children

The real meaning of this
Ancient Aryan symbol
The swastika
The Om
The creator's first word
For benediction

THE KITES

The tide is in
The ocean rests on its shoulders
A Greek tragedy
Enacted and buried in
Children's sandcastles
Tonight at last an amnesty
Agreed between men and the elements
In this deepening silence
Dogs bark and safely-returned soldiers
Fly kites attempting
To reach the other side
Perhaps peace will prevail
It has happened before

A VIEW OF THE WORLD FROM A HALF-OPEN WINDOW

Like the diplomacy of love
During the first meetings
The calculated words
The sideways grin with
Every smile
Half-projected commitments
With sips of something
Thoughts translating to
Controlled gazes into the future
Where dreams deposit
Their faith in a
Building Society account
I am looking at the world
From a half-open window
And enjoying it
Here
I hear no shouts
No comments
No media jerks
No regrets of
Wrongly typed texts
The world looks good today
With oceans of promises
I feel it's growing into me
Like a fragrance
Echoing like a symphony into
My veins and blood
I feel the presence of
Endless openings

I am falling in love
I want to sing today
In Sachmo's words
What a wonderful world

OBSERVING GRAVITY

Paul S. Higginbottom
Could have done that too
You know
He was only three apples away
But Isaac Newton had
To get the immortality

THE RESOLVE

I watched them
Singing their songs of love
Looking at their tattoos
All those names in them
The Catherines, the Elizabeths
The Dianas and Margarets
And then I listen to them
Chanting Rule Britannia
And Pakis go home
I see them polishing their helmets
Oiling their bikes
Dusting their gloves
Sharpening their knives
Demonstrating their kicks on a piece of brick
While looking at me
Etc etc etc
Yet I find myself
On every retreating day
Sitting in the same corner
In the coldest spot
With the resolve to survive
And I survive
And the next morning I get up
Wash
Offer my prayers and
Singing a popular hymn
Go to the shop
Open up the shutters
Switch on the lights
And look at the deposit books

And I feel satisfied
I smile
Pat my back
Well done son
You'll survive
And I do
And I stay
I hear some of them go
Down under

Satyendra Srivastava was born in Azamgarh, Uttar Pradesh, India in 1935. He was educated at the Universities of Poona and London, and has taught at the University of Toronto. Dr. Srivastava has been teaching at the University of Cambridge since 1980. He has lived in the U.K. for over thirty years.

He is the author of five previous collections of poetry in Hindi, and two plays. His *Mrs Jones aur vah gali* [Mrs Jones and Her Street] (1978) focuses on the evolution of a multi-cultural British community. He is a broadcaster and his journalism appears in the press in the U.K. and in India.